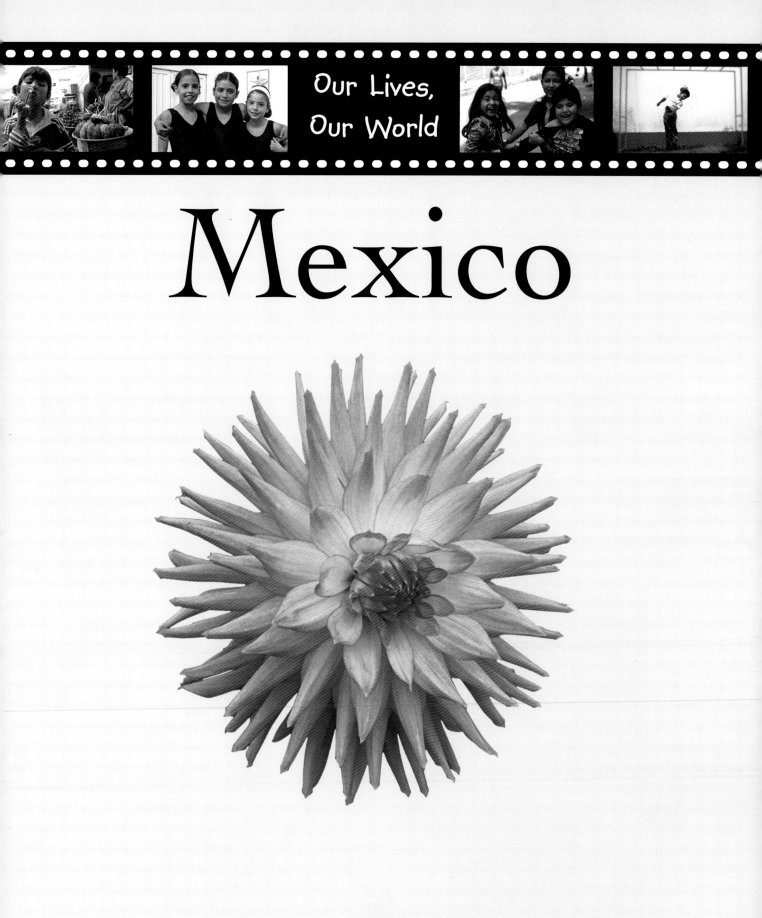

Our Lives,
Our World

Mexico

Chrysalis Children's Books

First published in the UK in 2005 by
Chrysalis Children's Books
An imprint of Chrysalis Books Group
The Chrysalis Building, Bramley Road
London W10 6SP

Copyright © Chrysalis Books Group Plc 2005

Compiled and edited by Susie Brooks
Associate Publisher: Joyce Bentley
Designed by: Tall Tree Books Ltd
Photographic consultant: Jenny Matthews
Photographic co-ordinators:
Gustavo Prado, Trisha Ziff
Picture researcher: Miguel Lamas
Translator: Gustavo Prado

ISBN 1 84458 191 8

Printed in China

10 9 8 7 6 5 4 3 2 1

British Library Cataloguing in Publication Data for
this book is available from the British Library.

The Publishers would like to thank the
photographers, Ramiro Chaves, Martha Miranda,
Fernando Montiel Klimt and Pavka Segura, for
capturing these wonderful children on film. Many
thanks also to Gustavo Prado of the Centro del
Imagen, Mexico City and Trisha Ziff, an independent
curator, for their support and encouragement
throughout the project.

Corbis: Eric Crichton Front Cover(BL), 1(BC), 5(BL),
Nik Wheeler 5(TL); Getty Images: Cosmo Condina 4(BR).

Contents

¡Hola! – Hello!

We are the children of Mexico and we can't
wait to share our lives with you in this book!

Welcome to Mexico!

We've got so much to show you! Let's start by telling you a bit about our country. We hope you'll come and see Mexico for yourself some time soon!

Our country

Mexico is part of North America. It is a long, ~~fairly~~ narrow country that stretches between the USA *in the north* and Guatemala and Belize in the south. To either ~~side~~ *both* sides of Mexico there is sea.

Popular beaches

The long coastlines mean that Mexico has some great beaches. They are very popular with tourists from all around the world.

A mountain capital

Mexico has lots of mountains. Some of these are volcanoes that still erupt sometimes. The Our capital, Mexico City, lies among mountains in the south of the country.

National flag

The stripes of our flag represent hope (green), purity (white) and the blood of our heroes (red). The eagle is a symbol of strength.

The climate

Summers in Mexico are very hot. In the north, winters are much cooler, but the south stays warm and humid. There is a rainy season that lasts from around June to October. Sometimes, dangerous winds called hurricanes hit the coasts.

National flower

Our national flower is the dahlia.

Speak Spanish!

hola – hello

adios – goodbye

por favor – please

gracias – thank you

Sol

Hi! My name is Sol Peresvarbosa Maceira – my first name means Sun! I am 9 years old and I live with my mum in Mexico City. My pet dog is called Diente, which means Tooth. It sounds fierce, but he's really very soft and cuddly!

"My friends say I'm so funny. I'm always telling jokes and making people laugh!"

I really love my mum, Frida. Our favourite thing is watching cartoons together on TV.

My parents are divorced but they are still good friends. Dad lives next door. He's an artist and he paints here in mum's house.

This is our house. It has a big garden and a great view of the mountains!

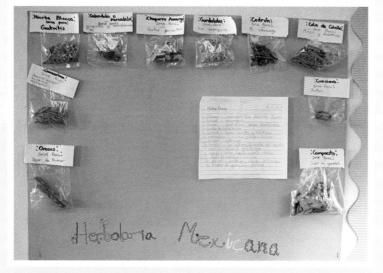

I go to school every day from Monday to Friday. Lessons start at 7.40am. My favourite subjects are history and art because they are the least boring!

Lots of herbs are grown here in Mexico. Doctors use some of them for medicine. We picked these ones on a class outing.

School days

Like most Mexican children, Sol goes to a large school for both boys and girls. She finishes around lunchtime and then has homework to do in the afternoon. Children in Mexico have to go to school until they are at least 16.

On Wednesday afternoons I go to ballet lessons. Here I am with two of my friends, - Florencia (left) and Alejandra.

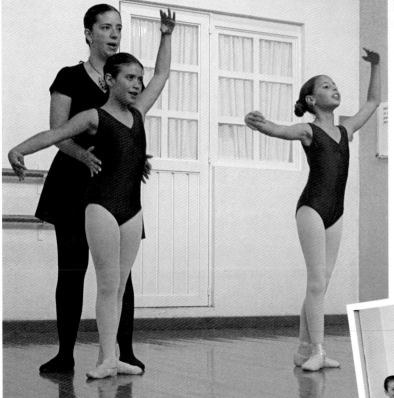

I love to dance - I've been learning now for two years!

Sometimes I help to teach the younger girls.

"When I grow up I want to be in a pop group or in the movies!"

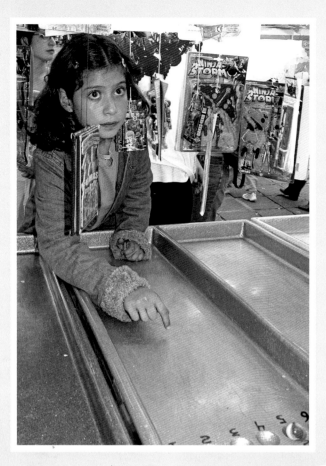

On special occasions a fair comes to our local square. I like playing marbles...

Spending money

In Mexico people spend pesos. Sol gets 10 pesos (about 60 pence) for pocket money every week, but not all families can afford this. Many Mexicans are very poor. Shopping in Mexico often means haggling to get a cheap price!

...and trying on earrings at the jewellery stalls. I usually try to save my pocket money, but I might spend some today!

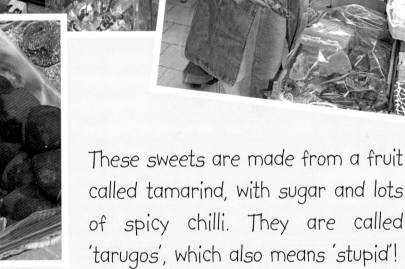

The sweet shop is another of my favourite places. I'm picking out traditional sweets to take to a party at school.

These sweets are made from a fruit called tamarind, with sugar and lots of spicy chilli. They are called 'tarugos', which also means 'stupid'!

Sweet celebrations

Mexicans love their sweets. There are hundreds of different sorts – most are made from natural ingredients that grow here, including fruits, nuts, pumpkin seeds, milk, coconut, chilli and even cacti! Sweets are popular during festivals such as Independence Day (15th/16th September) when stalls and fairs are set up all around the country.

Toño

Hello! My name's José Antonio Camacho Cova, but everyone calls me Toño. I'm 8 years old and I live with my mum, dad and brother in Cuauhtitlán, not far from Mexico City. Our home is in a block of flats that's owned by the government.

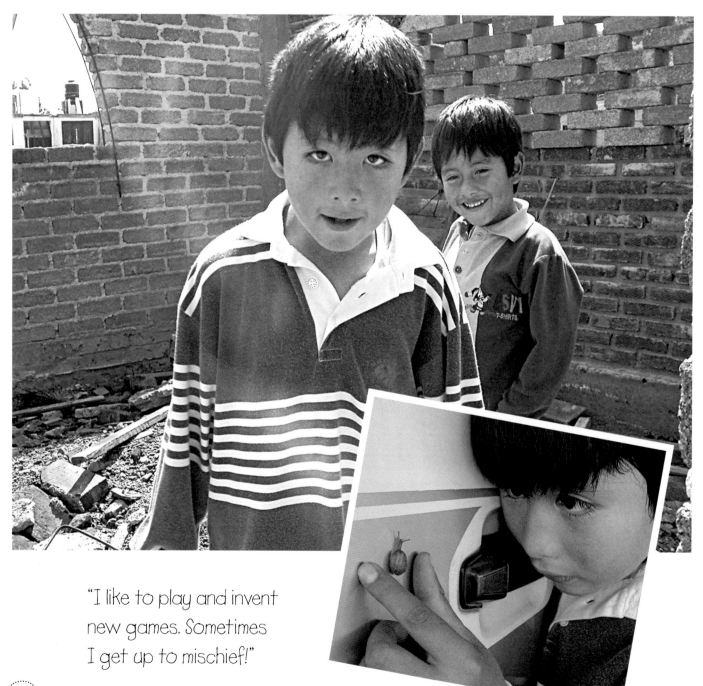

"I like to play and invent new games. Sometimes I get up to mischief!"

This is my family – my brother Fernando is 6. Dad's name is Fernando, too! And my mum is called Josefina.

Dad is a welder and an electrician. He also plays Mexican *salsa* music in a band. When I grow up I want to be like him – he's so cool!

My brother is my best friend – we're always happy when we're out mucking around together.

Dad used to live in Xochimilco, a place built on canals to the south of Mexico City. I love to go there and ride on the colourful boats.

Sometimes dad and his band rehearse their music here – I dance along! I'd like to play the drums, but everyone tells me I'm still too small.

We visit the local market to buy our food. We need some eggs, but Fernando and I wish we could take home a pet rabbit, too!

Amazing markets

Mexico's colourful street markets can sell anything from crafts and clothes to live animals. They are popular places for food shopping. All sorts of tropical fruits and vegetables grow well in Mexico's sunny climate, so there's plenty of choice. Big red chilli peppers, avocados, watermelons, oranges, mangoes, papayas and pineapples are just a few of the things to buy.

There are so many delicious fruits to choose from!

15

My favourite festival is Day of the Dead. We get to dress up as ghosts and skeletons and go around our neighbours' houses asking for money and sweets!

This is Fernando wearing his skeleton costume – spoooky!

Day of the Dead

On 2nd November – Day of the Dead – Mexicans take time to remember their relatives who have died. People visit family graves and set up altars in their homes, decorated with sugar skulls, photographs, and the favourite foods and belongings of the dead person. There are parties with music and feasts, to welcome the spirits of the dead back to earth.

At school we're all given candy skulls with our names on. We also eat special 'dead bread', which has bone shapes on top!

Saying prayers

Toño, like most Mexicans, is a Catholic. He believes in Jesus and the Virgin Mary and he prays every night to God the Holy Father. Many Mexican children also pray to their guardian angel to look after them and keep them well. They usually make a cross sign as they pray.

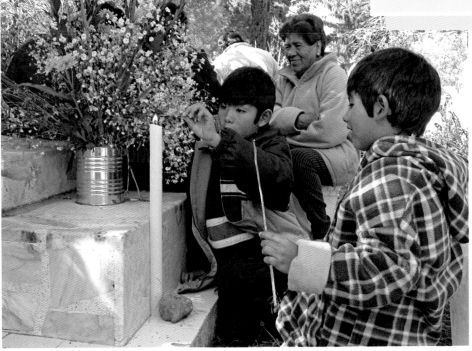

When we go to the graveyard we light candles, lay flowers and say a prayer. This is my uncle's grave. I remember fun times with him.

Noemi

Hola! I'm Noemi Samara Galván and I'm 7 years old. I live in a tiny apartment in a government block called 'Mermaids' – it's in Iztacalco, a part of Mexico City. My parents, grandparents, aunt, cousin and brother all live here too!

"I love Mexico because I really like our food, our parks, our festivals and our parties!"

This is my family, plus a couple of friends who live in the same block of flats. Our home has only two bedrooms so I share with mum, dad, my brother, my aunt and my cousin Fatima! My grandparents sleep in the other room.

Dad

Mum

Aunt Sairid

Gran

Brother Alfonso

Cousin Fatima

Mexico's people

Several cultures first lived in Mexico such as the Aztecs, the Zapotecs and the Mayans. Later, they were joined by settlers from Spain. Like Noemi, most Mexicans today are 'mestizos'. Mexico's official language is Spanish but there are also more than 60 indigenous languages, spoken in many Mexican villages that still remain today.

Gran is the most important person in my life. She is so full of love and she teaches me old Mexican songs!

Here we are outside our building. I'm not allowed to go far away on my own, but it's ok if Alfonso is with me.

"I like visiting the storytellers on the streets of Mexico City. We pay them 5 pesos to tell us a story!"

Sometimes we go to buy ice creams. My favourite is coffee flavour!

Most days we play outside with our friend Bryan who lives nearby.

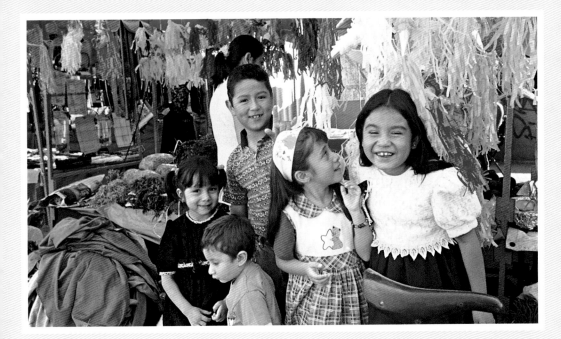

We all like visiting the toy stalls at the local market. My dad and grandfather sell things here.

I also love to dress up! This is my traditional costume – it's from a place called Michoacan in the north of Mexico. I normally wear it on Mother's Day on May 10th.

Colourful costumes

Most people in Mexico wear Western-style clothes, but on special occasions they may dress in traditional costumes. These usually include brightly woven or embroidered fabrics. Shawls, rebosos (shawls for warmth and carrying babies) and wide-brimmed hats called sombreros are popular. In some indigenous villages, people wear traditional clothing every day.

My school is in the housing area where I live, so it only takes me 4 minutes to walk there. This is my classroom.

I start lessons at 2.00pm and finish at 6.30pm. We have to wear a uniform with a tweed skirt, white shirt and navy sweater.

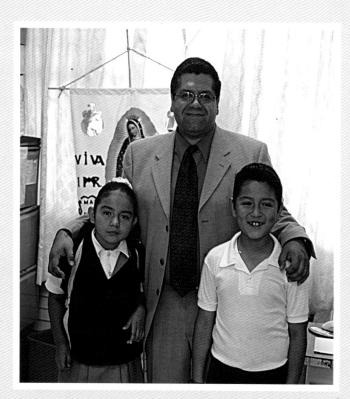

Alfonso goes to the same school. Here we are with our headmaster. We don't often visit his office – but he's glad to be in this book!

After school we eat dinner. My auntie cooks all sorts of typical Mexican foods, including eggs with refried beans, cheesy quesadillas, rice and belly of beef with chilli sauce! We also eat tortillas with avocados, and other Mexican fruits for dessert.

Tortillas and quesadillas

Tortillas are eaten everywhere in Mexico. These thin, flat breads are made of corn, the country's main crop. Tortillas are usually wrapped around foods such as meat, beans, avocado, cheese and vegetables. Quesadillas are stuffed tortillas that are baked and often served with spicy sauces.

Juan Pablo

Hi, I'm Juan Pablo García Miralrío – my surname means 'look at the river'! I'm 7 years old and I live with my parents and two brothers in Coatepec in the east of Mexico. I love my home, but I'd really like to visit Mexico City one day too!

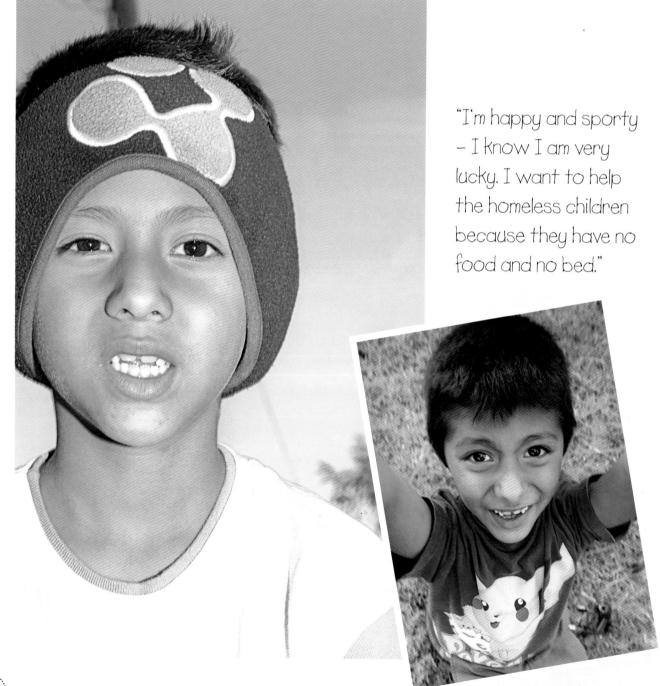

"I'm happy and sporty – I know I am very lucky. I want to help the homeless children because they have no food and no bed."

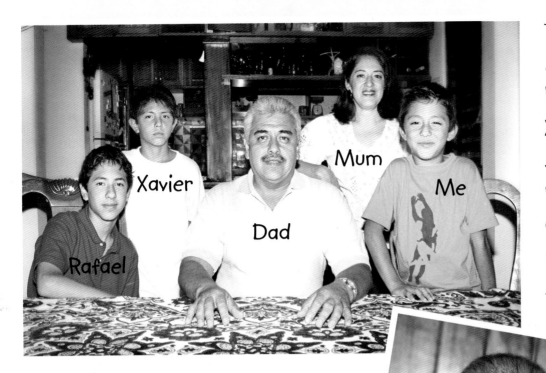

This is my family. My big brother Rafael is 14, and Xavier is 11. I share a bedroom with Xavier. He's always making me laugh with his silly jokes!

Dad is an architect. He built our house and most of the town we live in! Mum looks after me at home.

My naughty pet dog is called Coca Cola. She's wearing this bucket collar to stop her licking a wound.

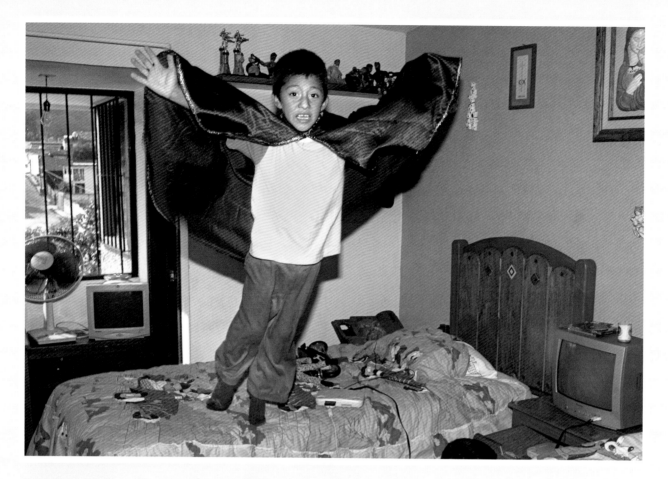

My friends all say I'm a little bit crazy! I like to play superhero...

...and mess around with my *bike*. It was so exciting when I first learnt how to ride it without stabilisers!

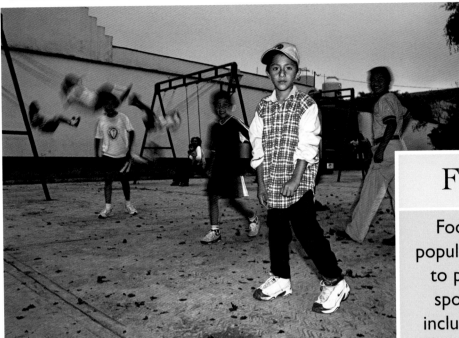

Sometimes I hang out with my friends at the local park.

Fun and games

Football is by far the most popular sport in Mexico – both to play and to watch. Other sports that Mexicans enjoy include baseball, wrestling and bullfighting. Dancing is also a popular pastime – traditional Mexican dances tend to be very fast and energetic!

"I've won medals for biking and for football, and certificates for doing tae kwon do!"

Football is my favourite sport – I'm a member of a local club. When I grow up I want to be a footballer because I love scoring goals so much!

We have some great toys in Mexico. These funny paper animals are called piñatas. They come in all sorts of shapes and they're full of suprises! I'm choosing one for my birthday party.

Piñatas

Mexican children's parties nearly all involve a piñata. It is a hollow model, usually made of papier mâché or cardboard, that is filled with treats such as sweets and small toys. Children take it in turns to beat the piñata with a stick while singing a special song – when it breaks the treats fall out!

In Mexico we say it's the game that is important, not the toy. So we often play with simple things, like spinning tops and yo-yos.

Lotería is a bit like bingo. A caller shouts the name of a card, or makes up a riddle about it, and you have to try to find it on your picture board. The first person to match a whole row of pictures wins!

I love these model wrestlers that we call 'luchadores'. I'm hoping to buy some more at this market stall.

Our Year

Here are some important events in our calendar!

JANUARY

Three Kings Day Many people receive presents today instead of on Christmas Day. We eat slices of a special cake called 'Rosca de Reyes', which has a little baby Jesus model baked inside.

Sol's birthday: 25th January

FEBRUARY

Candlemass Whoever got the baby Jesus in their piece of 'Rosca de Reyes' cake has to throw a party!

Flag Day We sing the national anthem and fly flags all around town.

MARCH

Birthday of Benito Juárez An official holiday when we remember the famous President who died in 1872. Around this date we also celebrate the arrival of spring.

Easter school holiday: 2 weeks in late March/early April

APRIL

Holy Week/Easter We build up to Easter with parades, prayers and parties. People break confetti-filled easter eggs over each other's heads!

MAY

Cinco de Mayo A national holiday in honour of Mexico's victory over the French who invaded in 1862.

Mother's Day We dress up in traditional costumes, dance, sing and give our mums cards and presents!

JULY

Guelaguetza Oaxaca (in southern Mexico) hosts a famous two-week festival of dancing, music and colourful parades.

Summer school holiday: 2 months from 1st July

AUGUST

Assumption Day An important date for Catholics, when we honour the Virgin Mary.

SEPTEMBER

Independence Day A huge festival celebrating Mexico's independence since 1810. The President rings a bell and shouts 'Long live Mexico' from the balcony of his palace. There are fireworks, fairs, parties, feasts and parades.

NOVEMBER/DECEMBER

Day of the Dead We make offerings, dress up and hold parties in memory of our dead relatives.
Posadas On any day between 16th and 24th December we re-enact the Christmas story and finish at a party with piñatas and punch.
Christmas Day We celebrate the birth of Jesus.

Toño's birthday: 1st November
Juan Pablo's birthday: 8th November
Noemi's birthday: 9th December

Christmas school holiday: December

¡Adios! – Goodbye!

Glossary

mestizo A Mexican with mixed Spanish and American Indian blood.

piñata A hollow papier-mâché toy that is filled with sweets and beaten with a stick until they fall out.

quesadilla A tortilla stuffed with meat or vegetables and baked or fried.

refried beans Beans that are boiled, mashed then fried.

resboso A shawl for warmth or to carry babies in.

salsa music A type of dance music that is popular in South and Central America.

sombrero A wide-brimmed hat, often made of straw.

tamarind A bitter tropical fruit that is used in cooking and in medicine.

tortilla A kind of thin, round pancake made from corn.

32

Index